VIOLIN

MW00668590

101 WORSHIP SONGS

Available for
FLUTE, CLARINET, ALTO SAX, TRUMPET, VIOLIN

ISBN 978-1-70512-282-2

HAL•LEONARD®

Visit Hal Leonard Online at **www.halleonard.com**

World headquarters, contact:
Hal Leonard
7777 West Bluemound Road
Milwaukee, WI 53213
Email: info@halleonard.com

In Europe, contact:
Hal Leonard Europe Limited
1 Red Place
London, W1K 6PL
Email: info@halleonardeurope.com

In Australia, contact:
Hal Leonard Australia Pty. Ltd.
4 Lentara Court
Cheltenham, Victoria, 3192 Australia
Email: info@halleonard.com.au

CONTENTS

4 Above All
5 Amazing Grace (My Chains Are Gone)
8 Ancient Words
6 Another in the Fire
13 As the Deer
9 At the Cross (Love Ran Red)
10 Battle Belongs
12 Because He Lives, Amen
15 Before the Throne of God Above
14 Blessed Be Your Name
16 The Blessing
18 Breathe
19 Broken Vessels (Amazing Grace)
20 Build My Life
22 Build Your Kingdom Here
24 Christ Our Hope in Life and Death
23 Come, Now Is the Time to Worship
26 Come Thou Fount, Come Thou King
27 Cornerstone
28 Days of Elijah
30 Do It Again
32 Draw Me Close
33 Everlasting God
34 Forever
35 Forever Reign
36 Give Thanks
25 Glorify Thy Name
38 Glorious Day
40 Good Good Father
37 Good Grace
42 Goodness of God
44 Graves into Gardens
50 Great Are You Lord
46 Great I Am
29 Great Is the Lord
48 Great Things
57 He Is Exalted
51 The Heart of Worship (When the Music Fades)
52 Here I Am to Worship (Light of the World)
53 His Mercy Is More
54 Holy Is the Lord
56 Holy Spirit
55 Hosanna (Praise Is Rising)
58 House of the Lord
31 How Deep the Father's Love for Us
60 How Great Is Our God
61 I Give You My Heart
62 I Will Rise

63 In Christ Alone
64 Indescribable
66 Is He Worthy?
68 Jesus Messiah
70 King of Kings
72 King of My Heart
73 Lamb of God
74 The Lion and the Lamb
76 Living Hope
87 Lord, I Lift Your Name on High
65 Lord, I Need You
78 Majesty
79 Mighty to Save
77 More Precious Than Silver
80 No Longer Slaves
81 Nothing Else
84 O Church Arise
82 O Come to the Altar
85 O Praise the Name (Anástasis)
86 Oceans (Where Feet May Fail)
90 One Thing Remains (Your Love Never Fails)
88 Only King Forever
91 Open the Eyes of My Heart
92 Open Up the Heavens
94 Our God
95 The Power of the Cross (Oh to See the Dawn)
96 Raise a Hallelujah
98 Reckless Love
100 Resurrecting
102 Revelation Song
104 Run to the Father
106 See a Victory
93 Shine, Jesus, Shine
103 Shine on Us
108 Shout to the Lord
109 Speak O Lord
109 Step by Step
114 10,000 Reasons (Bless the Lord)
111 There Is a Redeemer
110 This I Believe (The Creed)
112 This Is Amazing Grace
116 Way Maker
124 We Fall Down
118 What a Beautiful Name
120 Who You Say I Am
115 Whom Shall I Fear (God of Angel Armies)
121 Worthy Is the Lamb
122 Yes I Will
125 Yet Not I but Through Christ in Me
124 You Are My All in All
126 You Are My King (Amazing Love)
127 Your Grace Is Enough
128 Your Name

ABOVE ALL

VIOLIN

Words and Music by PAUL BALOCHE
and LENNY LeBLANC

Worshipfully

AMAZING GRACE
(My Chains Are Gone)

VIOLIN

Words by JOHN NEWTON
Traditional American Melody
Additional Words and Music by CHRIS TOMLIN
and LOUIE GIGLIO

ANOTHER IN THE FIRE

VIOLIN

Words and Music by
CHRIS DAVENPORT

To Coda
1.
2.
D.S. al Coda
CODA

ANCIENT WORDS

VIOLIN

Words and Music by
LYNN DeSHAZO

VIOLIN

AT THE CROSS
(Love Ran Red)

Words and Music by MATT REDMAN,
JONAS MYRIN, CHRIS TOMLIN,
ED CASH and MATT ARMSTRONG

BATTLE BELONGS

VIOLIN

Words and Music by PHIL WICKHAM
and BRIAN JOHNSON

Moderate Rock feel

3
1., 2.
3.

BECAUSE HE LIVES, AMEN

VIOLIN

Words and Music by WILLIAM J. GAITHER, GLORIA GAITHER, DANIEL CARSON, CHRIS TOMLIN, ED CASH, MATT MAHER and JASON INGRAM

Moderately

AS THE DEER

Words and Music by
MARTIN NYSTROM

BLESSED BE YOUR NAME

VIOLIN

Words and Music by MATT REDMAN
and BETH REDMAN

BEFORE THE THRONE OF GOD ABOVE

Words and Music by VIKKI COOK
and CHARITIE BANCROFT

THE BLESSING

VIOLIN

Words and Music by KARI JOBE CARNES,
CODY CARNES, STEVEN FURTICK
and CHRIS BROWN

1.
2.
2.
1.
2.

BREATHE

VIOLIN

Words and Music by
MARIE BARNETT

BROKEN VESSELS
(Amazing Grace)

VIOLIN

Words and Music by JOEL HOUSTON
and JONAS MYRIN

Moderately

BUILD MY LIFE

VIOLIN

Words and Music by MATT REDMAN, PAT BARRETT, BRETT YOUNKER, KARL MARTIN and KIRBY KAPLE

To Coda
1.
2.
D.S. al Coda
CODA
1.
2.

BUILD YOUR KINGDOM HERE

VIOLIN

Words and Music by
REND COLLECTIVE

COME, NOW IS THE TIME TO WORSHIP

VIOLIN

Words and Music by
BRIAN DOERKSEN

CHRIST OUR HOPE IN LIFE AND DEATH

VIOLIN

Words and Music by KEITH GETTY,
MATT BOSWELL, JORDAN KAUFLIN,
MATTHEW MERKER and MATT PAPA

GLORIFY THY NAME

Words and Music by
DONNA W. ADKINS

COME THOU FOUNT, COME THOU KING

VIOLIN

Traditional
Additional Words and Music by
THOMAS MILLER

CORNERSTONE

VIOLIN

Words and Music by JONAS MYRIN,
REUBEN MORGAN, ERIC LILJERO
and EDWARD MOTE

DAYS OF ELIJAH

VIOLIN

Words and Music by
ROBIN MARK

GREAT IS THE LORD

Words and Music by MICHAEL W. SMITH
and DEBORAH D. SMITH

DO IT AGAIN

VIOLIN

Words and Music by MATT REDMAN,
STEVEN FURTICK, CHRIS BROWN
and MACK BROCK

Moderately

HOW DEEP THE FATHER'S LOVE FOR US

Words and Music by
STUART TOWNEND

Quietly

DRAW ME CLOSE

VIOLIN

Words and Music by
KELLY CARPENTER

EVERLASTING GOD

VIOLIN

Words and Music by BRENTON BROWN
and KEN RILEY

FOREVER

VIOLIN

Words and Music by
CHRIS TOMLIN

FOREVER REIGN

VIOLIN

Words and Music by JASON INGRAM
and REUBEN MORGAN

GIVE THANKS

VIOLIN

Words and Music by
HENRY SMITH

GOOD GRACE

VIOLIN

Words and Music by
JOEL HOUSTON

GLORIOUS DAY

VIOLIN

Words and Music by SEAN CURRAN,
KRISTIAN STANFILL, JASON INGRAM
and JONATHAN SMITH

1.
2.

GOOD GOOD FATHER

VIOLIN

Words and Music by PAT BARRETT
and ANTHONY BROWN

1.
2.
D.S. al Coda
CODA

GOODNESS OF GOD

VIOLIN

Words and Music by BEN FIELDING, ED CASH, JASON INGRAM, JENN JOHNSON and BRIAN JOHNSON

Moderately slow

GRAVES INTO GARDENS

VIOLIN

Words and Music by CHRIS BROWN,
STEVEN FURTICK, TIFFANY HAMMER
and BRANDON LAKE

Joyfully, in 2

2.
1.
2.
1.
2.

GREAT I AM

VIOLIN

Words and Music by
JARED ANDERSON

Moderate Pop beat

1.
2.

GREAT THINGS

VIOLIN

Words and Music by JONAS MYRIN
and PHIL WICKHAM

1.
2.
1.
2.

GREAT ARE YOU LORD

VIOLIN

Words and Music by JASON INGRAM,
DAVID LEONARD and LESLIE JORDAN

THE HEART OF WORSHIP

(When the Music Fades)

VIOLIN

Words and Music by
MATT REDMAN

Steady Ballad

HERE I AM TO WORSHIP
(Light of the World)

VIOLIN

Words and Music by
TIM HUGHES

Moderately slow, steady

HIS MERCY IS MORE

VIOLIN

Words and Music by MATT BOSWELL
and MATT PAPA

HOLY IS THE LORD

VIOLIN

Words and Music by CHRIS TOMLIN
and LOUIE GIGLIO

HOSANNA
(Praise Is Rising)

VIOLIN

Words and Music by PAUL BALOCHE
and BRENTON BROWN

Moderately fast

HOLY SPIRIT

VIOLIN

Words and Music by KATIE TORWALT
and BRYAN TORWALT

Worship Ballad

HE IS EXALTED

Words and Music by
TWILA PARIS

HOUSE OF THE LORD

VIOLIN

Words and Music by PHIL WICKHAM
and JONATHAN SMITH

D.S. al Coda
CODA
3
3
3
1.
3
2.
1.
2.

HOW GREAT IS OUR GOD

VIOLIN

Words and Music by CHRIS TOMLIN,
JESSE REEVES and ED CASH

I GIVE YOU MY HEART

VIOLIN

Words and Music by
REUBEN MORGAN

I WILL RISE

VIOLIN

Words and Music by CHRIS TOMLIN,
JESSE REEVES, LOUIE GIGLIO
and MATT MAHER

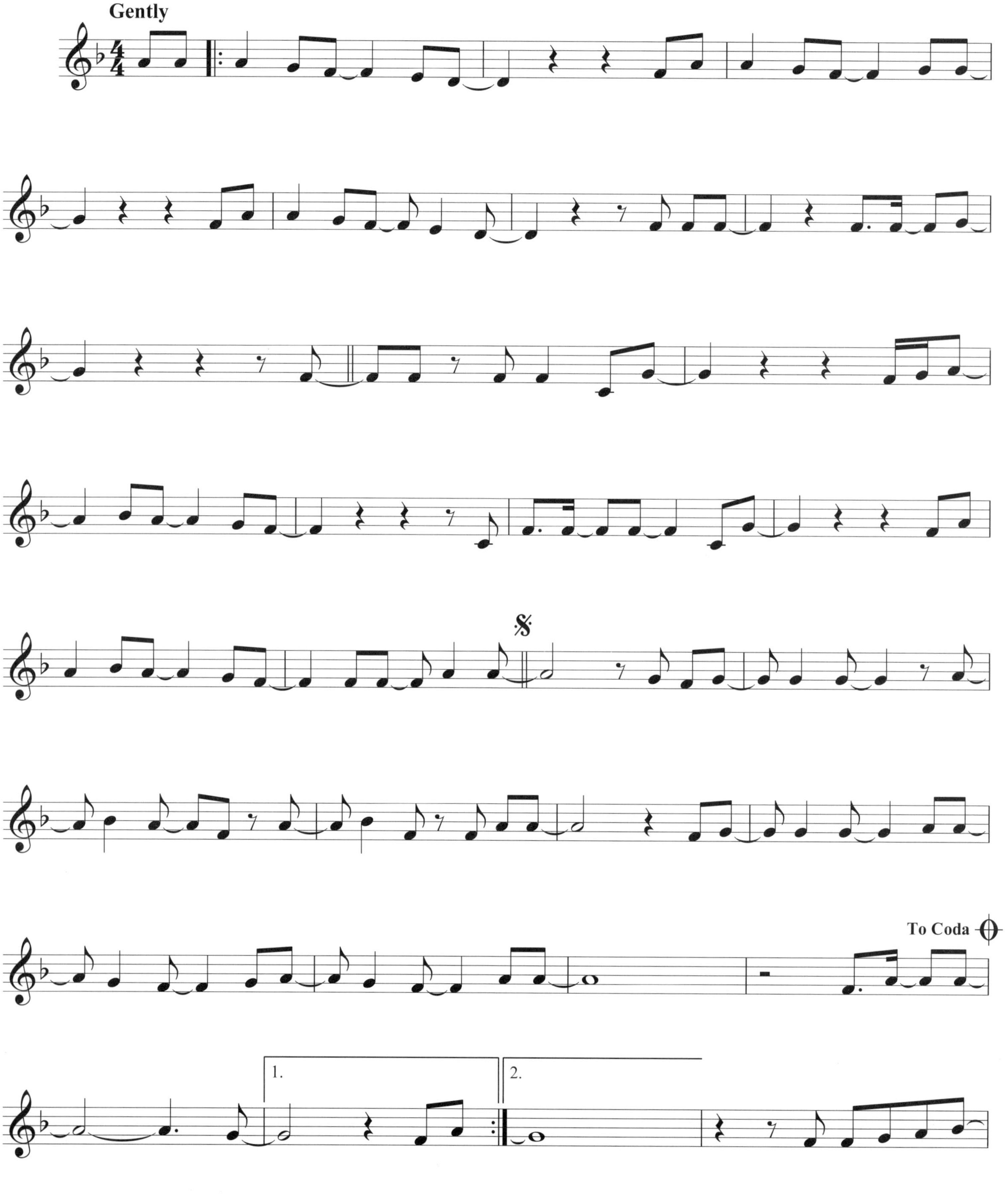

IN CHRIST ALONE

Words and Music by KEITH GETTY
and STUART TOWNEND

INDESCRIBABLE

VIOLIN

Words and Music by LAURA STORY
and JESSE REEVES

LORD, I NEED YOU

VIOLIN

Words and Music by JESSE REEVES,
KRISTIAN STANFILL, MATT MAHER,
CHRISTY NOCKELS and DANIEL CARSON

IS HE WORTHY?

VIOLIN

Words and Music by ANDREW PETERSON
and BEN SHIVE

D.S. al Coda
CODA

JESUS MESSIAH

VIOLIN

Words and Music by CHRIS TOMLIN,
JESSE REEVES, DANIEL CARSON
and ED CASH

Moderately

1.
2.

KING OF KINGS

VIOLIN

Words and Music by SCOTT LIGERTWOOD,
BROOKE LIGERTWOOD and JASON INGRAM

Moderately

KING OF MY HEART

VIOLIN

Words and Music by JOHN MARK McMILLAN
and SARAH McMILLAN

LAMB OF GOD

Words and Music by
TWILA PARIS

With emotion

THE LION AND THE LAMB

VIOLIN

Words and Music by BRENTON BROWN,
BRIAN JOHNSON and LEELAND MOORING

1.
2.
D.S. al Coda
CODA
1.
2.

LIVING HOPE

VIOLIN

Words and Music by PHIL WICKHAM
and BRIAN JOHNSON

MORE PRECIOUS THAN SILVER

Words and Music by
LYNN DeSHAZO

MAJESTY

VIOLIN

Words and Music by
JACK HAYFORD

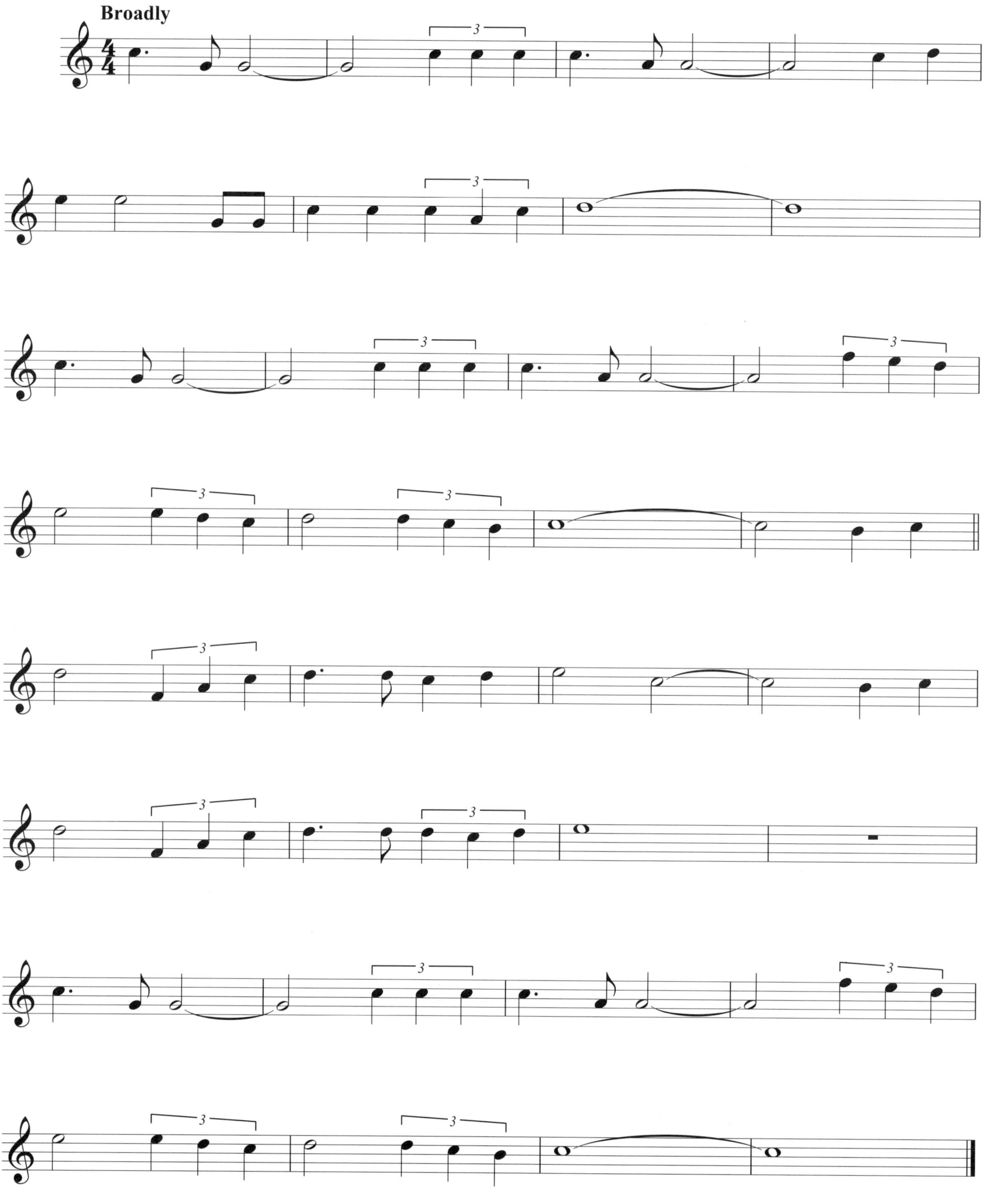

MIGHTY TO SAVE

VIOLIN

Words and Music by BEN FIELDING
and REUBEN MORGAN

NO LONGER SLAVES

VIOLIN

Words and Music by JONATHAN DAVID HELSER,
BRIAN JOHNSON and JOEL CASE

NOTHING ELSE

VIOLIN

Words and Music by CODY CARNES,
HANK BENTLEY and JESSIE EARLY

O COME TO THE ALTAR

VIOLIN

Words and Music by CHRIS BROWN,
MACK BROCK, STEVEN FURTICK
and WADE JOYE

D.S. al Coda
CODA
1.
2.
1.
2.

O CHURCH ARISE

VIOLIN

Words and Music by KEITH GETTY
and STUART TOWNEND

O PRAISE THE NAME
(Anástasis)

VIOLIN

Words and Music by MARTY SAMPSON,
BENJAMIN HASTINGS and DEAN USSHER

VIOLIN

OCEANS

(Where Feet May Fail)

Words and Music by JOEL HOUSTON,
MATT CROCKER and SALOMON LIGHTHELM

LORD, I LIFT YOUR NAME ON HIGH

Words and Music by
RICK FOUNDS

ONLY KING FOREVER

VIOLIN

Words and Music by MACK BROCK,
CHRISTOPHER BROWN, STEVEN FURTICK
and WADE JOYE

Joyfully, with a driving beat

To Coda
D.C. al Coda
CODA
1.
2.

ONE THING REMAINS

(Your Love Never Fails)

Words and Music by JEREMY RIDDLE,
BRIAN JOHNSON and CHRISTA BLACK

OPEN THE EYES OF MY HEART

VIOLIN

Words and Music by
PAUL BALOCHE

Moderately fast

OPEN UP THE HEAVENS

VIOLIN

Words and Music by JASON INGRAM, STUART GARRARD, ANDI ROZIER, JAMES MACDONALD and MEREDITH ANDREWS

SHINE, JESUS, SHINE

VIOLIN

Words and Music by
GRAHAM KENDRICK

OUR GOD

VIOLIN

Words and Music by JONAS MYRIN, JESSE REEVES, CHRIS TOMLIN and MATT REDMAN

THE POWER OF THE CROSS

(Oh to See the Dawn)

Words and Music by STUART TOWNEND and KEITH GETTY

Moderately slow

RAISE A HALLELUJAH

VIOLIN

Words and Music by JONATHAN DAVID HELSER,
MELISSA HELSER, MOLLY SKAGGS
and JAKE STEVENS

Moderate Rock beat

1.
2.
1.
2.

RECKLESS LOVE

VIOLIN

Words and Music by CALEB CULVER,
CORY ASBURY and RAN JACKSON

1.
2., 3.
Fine
D.S. al Fine
(take 2nd ending)

RESURRECTING

VIOLIN

Words and Music by CHRIS BROWN,
MACK BROCK, STEVEN FURTICK,
WADE JOYE and MATTHEWS THABO NTELE

To Coda
D.S. al Coda
CODA

REVELATION SONG

VIOLIN

Words and Music by
JENNIE LEE RIDDLE

SHINE ON US

Words and Music by MICHAEL W. SMITH
and DEBBIE SMITH

RUN TO THE FATHER

VIOLIN

Words and Music by RAN JACKSON,
MATT MAHER and CODY CARNES

1.
2.

SEE A VICTORY

VIOLIN

Words and Music by CHRIS BROWN,
STEVEN FURTICK, JASON INGRAM
AND BEN FIELDING

CODA

SHOUT TO THE LORD

VIOLIN

Words and Music by
DARLENE ZSCHECH

Worshipfully

SPEAK O LORD

VIOLIN

Words and Music by STUART TOWNEND
and KEITH GETTY

Prayerfully

STEP BY STEP

Words and Music by
DAVID STRASSER "BEAKER"

Moderately fast

VIOLIN

THIS I BELIEVE
(The Creed)

Words and Music by BEN FIELDING
and MATT CROCKER

THERE IS A REDEEMER

Words and Music by
MELODY GREEN

Moderately

THIS IS AMAZING GRACE

VIOLIN

Words and Music by PHIL WICKHAM,
JOSHUA NEIL FARRO and JEREMY RIDDLE

D.S. al Coda
CODA

VIOLIN

10,000 REASONS
(Bless the Lord)

Words and Music by JONAS MYRIN
and MATT REDMAN

WHOM SHALL I FEAR
(God of Angel Armies)

VIOLIN

Words and Music by CHRIS TOMLIN, ED CASH and SCOTT CASH

WAY MAKER

VIOLIN

Words and Music by
OSINACHI KALU OKORO EGBU

1.
2.
D.S. al Coda
CODA

WHAT A BEAUTIFUL NAME

VIOLIN

Words and Music by BEN FIELDING
and BROOKE LIGERTWOOD

Moderately slow

1.
2.
To Coda
D.S. al Coda
CODA

WHO YOU SAY I AM

VIOLIN

Words and Music by REUBEN MORGAN
and BEN FIELDING

WORTHY IS THE LAMB

VIOLIN

Words and Music by
DARLENE ZSCHECH

YES I WILL

VIOLIN

Words and Music by MIA FIELDES,
EDDIE HOAGLAND and JONATHAN SMITH

WE FALL DOWN

Words and Music by
CHRIS TOMLIN

Worshipfully

YOU ARE MY ALL IN ALL

By DENNIS JERNIGAN

Moderately

YET NOT I BUT THROUGH CHRIST IN ME

VIOLIN

Words and Music by MICHAEL FARREN,
JONNY ROBINSON and RICH THOMPSON

VIOLIN

YOU ARE MY KING
(Amazing Love)

Words and Music by
BILLY JAMES FOOTE

YOUR GRACE IS ENOUGH

VIOLIN

Words and Music by
MATT MAHER

YOUR NAME

VIOLIN

Words and Music by PAUL BALOCHE
and GLENN PACKIAM